A
Rookie
reader®

LOOK FOR LADYBUGS

Written by Dana Meachen Rau
Illustrated by Christine Schneider

Children's Press®
A Division of Scholastic Inc.
New York • Toronto • London • Auckland • Sydney
Mexico City • New Delhi • Hong Kong
Danbury, Connecticut

To Emmeline, my little bookworm
—C. S.

Reading Consultant

Cecilia Minden-Cupp, PhD
Former Director of the Language and Literacy Program
Harvard Graduate School of Education
Cambridge, Massachusetts

Cover design: The Design Lab
Interior design: Herman Adler

Library of Congress Cataloging-in-Publication Data

Rau, Dana Meachen, 1971–
 Look for ladybugs / by Dana Meachen Rau ; illustrated by Christine Schneider.
  p. cm. — (A rookie reader)
 Summary: Simple, rhyming text about a ladybug search teaches about
prepositional phrases.
 ISBN 10: 0-531-12470-3 (lib. bdg.)   0-531-12493-2 (pbk.)
 ISBN 13: 978-0-531-12470-3 (lib. bdg.)   978-0-531-12493-2 (pbk.)
 [1. Ladybugs—Fiction. 2. English language—Prepositions—Fiction.
3. Stories in rhyme.] I. Schneider, Christine, 1971– ill. II. Title. III. Series.
 PZ8.3.R232Loo 2006
 [E]—dc22   2006006756

CHILDREN'S PRESS, and A ROOKIE READER®, and associated logos
are trademarks and/or registered trademarks of Scholastic Library
Publishing. SCHOLASTIC and associated logos are trademarks and/or
registered trademarks of Scholastic Inc.
1 2 3 4 5 6 7 8 9 10 R 16 15 14 13 12 11 10 09 08 07

Let's look for ladybugs!

3

Where do they hide?

Look by the window.

7

Look down the slide.

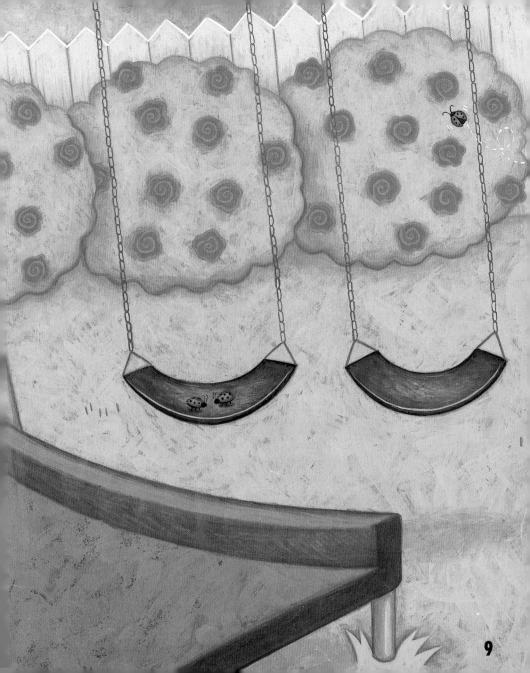

Look for ladybugs up in the sky.

10

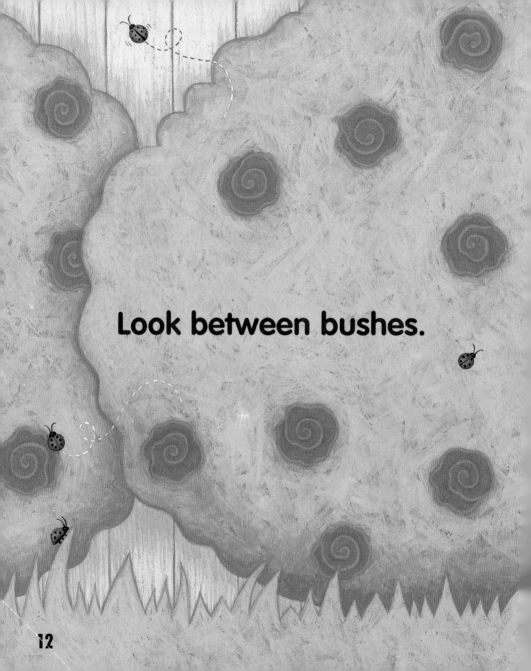

Look between bushes.

Look low and high.

Look for ladybugs along the wall.

Look behind trash cans.

18

19

Look on the ball.

Look for ladybugs under the mat.

Look through a log.

Look near the cat.

Look for ladybugs up in a tree.

Find a ladybug sitting on me!

Word List (40 words)
(Words in **bold** are prepositions.)

a	do	log	the
along	**down**	look	they
and	find	low	**through**
ball	**for**	mat	trash
behind	hide	me	tree
between	high	**near**	**under**
bushes	**in**	**on**	**up**
by	ladybug	sitting	wall
cans	ladybugs	sky	where
cat	let's	slide	window

About the Author

Dana Meachen Rau loves her backyard in Burlington, Connecticut. She sees ladybugs there, as well as squirrels, birds, turtles, and butterflies. Inside her house, Dana writes. She has written more than 150 children's books, including many early readers.

About the Illustrator

Christine M. Schneider writes and illustrates for kids in her home studio in Lawrence, Kansas. She hunts for ladybugs, caterpillars, and fireflies in her garden with her husband, her daughter, and their two cats. This is the seventh book she has illustrated.